# Psalms, Hymns & Spiritual Songs

## Volume 1

*Psalms, Hymns
and Spiritual Songs*
*Volume 1*

*Hymns of Grace*
hymnsofgrace.org

Editor: Philip Webb
Engraving: Dan Kreider
Design: Matthew Wahl
© 2024 Grace Community Church
13248 Roscoe Blvd.
Los Angeles, CA 91352

ISBN 979-8-9887200-1-0
Item #PHSS001

# A Mighty Fortress Is Our God

C    Csus   C   F    Gsus   C

1. A might-y for-tress is our God, a bul-wark nev-er fail - ing;
2. Did we in our own strength con-fide, our striv-ing would be los - ing,
3. And tho' this world with dev-ils filled should threat-en to un-do us,
4. That word a-bove all earth-ly pow'rs, no thanks to them, a - bid - eth;

C    Csus   Am   F    Gsus   C

our Help-er He, a - mid the flood of mor-tal ills pre - vail - ing.
were not the right Man on our side, the Man of God's own choos - ing.
we will not fear, for God hath willed His truth to tri-umph through us.
the Spir - it and the gifts are ours through Him who with us sid - eth.

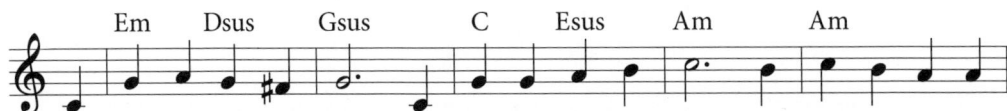

Em   Dsus   Gsus   C   Esus   Am   Am

For still our an-cient foe doth seek to work us woe; his craft and pow'r are
Dost ask who that may be? Christ Je-sus, it is He! Lord Sab-a-oth His
The prince of dark-ness grim, we trem-ble not for him; his rage we can en-
Let goods and kin-dred go, this mor-tal life al - so; the bod-y they may

Em   F   Esus   Am   F   Gsus   C

great, and, armed with cru - el hate; on earth is not his e - qual.
name, from age to age the same, and He must win the bat - tle.
dure, for lo, his doom is sure; one lit - tle word shall fell him.
kill: God's truth a - bid-eth still— His king-dom is for-ev - er!

Words: Martin Luther, 1529; tr. Frederick Hedge, 1853  
Music: Martin Luther, 1529

EIN' FESTE BURG  
87 87 66 66 7

# All Creatures of Our God and King

C         Am

1. All crea - tures of our God and King,    lift up your
2. Let all things their Cre - a - tor bless    and wor - ship
3. All the re - deemed washed by His blood,    come and re -
4. He shall re - turn in pow'r to reign,    heav - en and

F

voice and with us sing,    O praise Him!    Al - le - lu - ia!
Him in hum - ble - ness.    O praise Him!    Al - le - lu - ia!
joice in His great love.    O praise Him!    Al - le - lu - ia!
earth will join to say,    O praise Him!    Al - le - lu - ia!

C         Am

Thou, burn - ing sun with gold - en beam,    thou, sil - ver moon with
Praise, praise the Fa - ther, praise the Son,    and praise the Spir - it,
Christ has de - feat - ed ev - 'ry sin,    cast all your bur - dens
Then who shall fall on bend - ed knee?    All crea - tures of our

F         C/E

soft - er gleam,
Three in One!    O praise Him!    O praise Him!
now on Him.
God and King.

F      Am      G   F

Al - le - lu - ia!    Al - le - lu - ia!    Al - le - lu - ia!

Words: St. Francis of Assisi, vs. 1–2; trans. William Henry Draper
Music: 16th cent. German tune; adapt. Jonathan Baird and Ryan Baird, vs. 3–4
© 2013 Sovereign Grace Worship

# Ancient of Days

1. Though the na-tions rage, king-doms rise and fall, there is still one
2. Though the dread of night o-ver-whelms my soul, He is here with
3. Though I may not see what the fu-ture brings, I will watch and

King reign-ing o-ver all. So I will not fear for this truth re-
me— I am not a-lone. O His love is sure, and He knows my
wait for the Sav-ior King. Then, my joy com-plete, stand-ing face to

mains: that my God is the An-cient of Days.
name, for my God is the An-cient of Days. None a-bove Him,
face in the pre-sence of the An-cient of Days.

none be-fore Him; all of time in His hands. For His throne, it shall re-

main and ev-er stand. All the pow-er, all the glo-ry, I will

trust in His name, for my God is the An-cient of Days.

Words and Music: Jonny Robinson, Rich Thompson, Michael Farren, and Jesse Reeves © 2018 CityAlight Music

# Behold Our God

1. Who has held the o-ceans in His hands? Who has num-bered
2. Who has giv-en coun-sel to the Lord? Who can ques-tion
3. Who has felt the nails up-on His hands, bear-ing all the

ev-'ry grain of sand? Kings and na-tions trem-ble at His voice;
an-y of His words? Who can teach the One who knows all things?
guilt of sin-ful man? God e-ter-nal, hum-bled to the grave;

*Chorus*

all cre-a-tion ris-es to re-joice!
Who can fath-om all His won-drous deeds? Be-hold our
Je-sus, Sav-ior, ris-en now to reign!

God, seat-ed on His throne: come, let us a-dore Him! Be-hold our

*3rd time to Bridge*

King! Noth-ing can com-pare; come, let us a-dore Him!

Words and Music: Stephen Altrogge, Jonathan Baird, Ryan Baird, and Meghan Baird

Bridge
C F
Let Your glo - ry fill the earth,
You will reign for - ev - er,
C F Am
let Your glo - ry fill the earth, let Your
You will reign for - ev - er, You will reign for -
F Am F to Chorus
glo - ry fill the earth, let Your glo - ry fill. Be -
ev - er, You will reign for - ev - er!

# From Everlasting (Psalm 90)

1. O God, be - fore the moun-tains were brought forth, or
2. We dwell be - neath the stars in an - cient skies, a
3. O God, when joy and trag - e - dy col - lide and

days of spring and sum-mer filled the earth, from ev - er - last - ing,
thou-sand years are noth-ing in Your sight, from ev - er - last - ing,
loss re-minds us life is but a sigh, from ev - er - last - ing,

You are God.
You are God. And all our days are held with-in Your hands,
You are God.

Your per-fect love and fa-vor have no end. We rest with-in the

wis-dom of Your plan, ev - er - last - ing God.

4. O God of light, our ways are known to You, but by Your grace You're

**Eb2** ... **Bb/D**

mak-ing all things new, so sat-is-fy us in our num-bered

**Eb2** ... **Bb/F** ... **Eb2/G**

days, es-tab-lish ev-'ry ef-fort while we wait. From ev-er-

**Gm7** ... **Eb** ... **Bb** **F/A** ... **Gm**

last - ing, You are God. And all our days are

**Eb** ... **Bb** ... **F**

held with-in Your hands, Your per-fect love and fa-vor have no end.

**Gm** ... **Eb** ... **Bb/D** **F**

We rest with-in the wis-dom of Your plan, ev-er-last-ing, and

**Gm** ... **Eb** ... **Bb** ... **Eb2**

all our days are held with-in Your hands, Your per-fect love and fa-vor have no

**Gm7** **F** **Gm** ... **Eb** ... **Bb/F** **F** **Bb**

end. We rest with-in the wis-dom of Your plan, ev-er-last-ing God.

# Before the Throne of God Above

| D | Dsus | D | Bm |

1. Be - fore the throne of God a - bove    I have a strong and per - fect
2. When Sa -tan tempts me  to  de - spair,  and tells me  of  the guilt with-
3. Be -hold Him there, the  ris - en Lamb!  My per - fect, spot - less Right-eous-

| F#m | G | Asus | Bm |

plea,    a great High Priest  whose name is  Love,    who  ev - er
in,    up- ward I    look    and    see Him there    who made an
ness;   the great un - change - a -  ble I   AM,    the King of

| G | D/A | D | D/F# | G | A |

lives and pleads for    me.    My name is  grav - en  on His  hands;
end  to  all   my    sin.    Be - cause the  sin - less Sav - ior  died,
glo - ry and   of    grace!  One with Him - self  I   can- not   die;

| D/F# | G | Bm | Bm/A |

my name  is    writ - ten    on His    heart;    I  know that
my sin - ful   soul    is    count - ed    free;    for God  the
my soul  is    pur - chased   with His   blood;    my  life   is

| G | Asus | Bm | G |

while   in   heav'n He stands,   no tongue can  bid me thence  de -
Just    is   sat - is - fied    to   look   on   Him and  par - don
hid    with  Christ on  high,   with Christ  my   Sav - ior  and   my

| Bm | G | D |

part;    no tongue can  bid  me thence   de -  part.
me;    to   look   on   Him and  par - don    me.
God;    with Christ  my   Sav - ior   and    my    God!

Words: Charitie Lees Smith, alternate lyrics by Vikki Cook
Music: Vikki Cook © 1997 Sovereign Grace Worship

# God Is for Us

1. We won't fear the bat-tle, we won't fear the night; we will walk the val-ley,
2. E-ven when I stum-ble, e-ven when I fall, e-ven when I turn back,

with You by our side. You will go be-fore us, You will lead the way;
still Your love is sure. You will not a-ban-don, You will not for-sake;

we have found a ref-uge, on-ly You can save. Sing with joy now,
You will cheer me on-ward with nev-er end-ing grace.

our God is for us; the Fa-ther's love is a strong and might-y for-tress.

Raise your voice now, no love is great-er. Who can stand a-gainst us if our

*2nd time to Bridge*
*Last time end*

God is for us?

*Bridge*

Nei-ther height nor depth can sep-ar-ate us; hell and

*2nd time to Chorus*

death will not de-feat us. He who gave His Son to free us holds me in His love.

Words and Music: Michael Farren, James Ferguson, Tiarne Tranter, Jesse Reeves, Jonny Robinson, James Tealy, and Rich Thompson © 2018 CityAlight Music

# How Majestic Is Your Name (Psalm 8)

1. When I look at Your heav-ens, the moon and stars You set in mo-tion, oh, God, I sing all glo-ry and hon-or. What is man that You are mind-ful? The son of man, that You would care for him? We sing all glo-ry and hon-or. Oh, LORD, our Lord, oh, how awe-some are Your ways. How maj-es-tic is Your name in all the earth. Oh, LORD, our Lord, may we see Your king-dom come. Fa-ther, may Your will be done in all the earth.

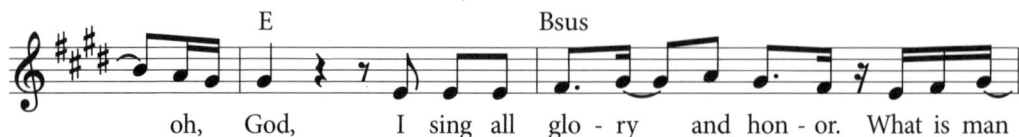

*Chorus*

*2nd time to Coda*
*Last time end*

Words and Music: Shane Barnard © 2020 Songs from the Wellhouse

2. In all the earth, You gave do - min - ion to Your chil - dren,

and You crowned them, oh, God, with glo - ry and hon - or.

So we'll sing of Your Name, live our lives for Your great - ness,

oh, God, and Your glo - ry and hon - or. Oh, LORD,

**⊕ Coda**

(earth). The earth is full of the glo - ry of God.

Come, make much of the Name a - bove all names. Cre - a - tion

*to Chorus*

cries out, and ev - 'ry knee bows. Je - sus, we crown You

oh, LORD, our Lord. Oh, LORD, our Lord.

# How Great Thou Art

1. O Lord my God, when I in awe-some won-der con-sid-er
2. And when I think that God, His Son not spar-ing, sent Him to
3. When Christ shall come with shout of ac-cla-ma-tion and take me

all the worlds Thy hands have made, I see the stars, I hear the roll-ing
die, I scarce can take it in, that on the cross, my bur-den glad-ly
home, what joy shall fill my heart! Then I shall bow in hum-ble ad-o-

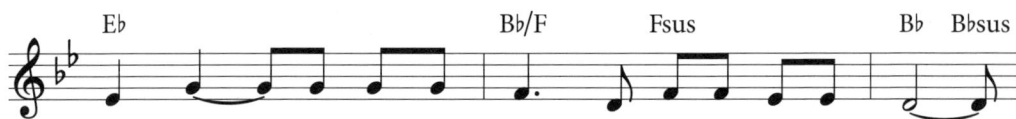

thun-der, Thy pow'r through-out the u-ni-verse dis-played.
bear-ing, He bled and died to take a-way my sin.
ra-tion, and there pro-claim, "My God, how great Thou art!"

Then sings my soul, my Sav-ior God, to Thee: how great Thou art,

how great Thou art! Then sings my soul, my Sav-ior God, to

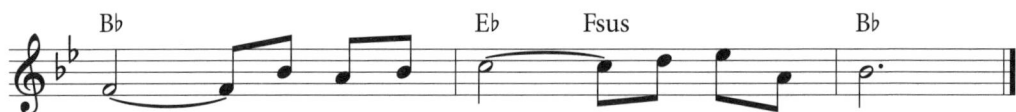

Thee: how great Thou art, how great Thou art!

Words: Stuart K. Hine, 1949; Music: Swedish folk melody, adapt. and arr. Stuart K. Hine

# Holy, Holy, Holy

C5        F/C        C

1. Ho - ly, ho - ly, ho - ly! Lord God Al - might - y!
2. Ho - ly, ho - ly, ho - ly! all the saints a - dore Thee,
3. Ho - ly, ho - ly, ho - ly! though the dark - ness hide Thee,
4. Ho - ly, ho - ly, ho - ly! Lord God Al - might - y!

G/B      Am   G/B   C/D   Dsus

Ear - ly in the morn - ing our song shall rise to
cast - ing down their gold - en crowns a - round the glass - y
though the eye of sin - ful man Thy glo - ry may not
All Thy works shall praise Thy name, in earth and sky and

G  C5             F/C

Thee; ho - ly, ho - ly, ho - ly, mer - ci - ful and
sea; cher - u - bim and ser - a - phim, fall - ing down be -
see; on - ly Thou art ho - ly, there is none be -
sea; ho - ly, ho - ly, ho - ly, mer - ci - ful and

C G/B Am C/E  Fmaj7   F   Gsus   C

might - y! God in three Per - sons, bless - ed Trin - i - ty!
fore Thee, who was and is, and ev - er - more shall be.
side Thee, per - fect in pow'r, in love, and pu - ri - ty.
might - y! God in three Per - sons, bless - ed Trin - i - ty!

Words: Reginald Heber, 1826
Music: John B. Dykes, 1861

NICAEA
11 12 12 10

# Praise the Lord (Psalm 150)

**G**

1. You made the star - ry hosts, You traced the moun-tain peaks, You
2. You reached in - to the dust, in love Your Spir - it breathed; You
3. Let sym - pho-nies re - sound, let drums and choirs ring out, all

**C/G**

**G**      **C/G**    **G**

paint the eve-ning sky with won - ders. The earth, it is Your throne,
formed us in Your ver - y like - ness to know Your won-drous works,
heav - en hear the sound of wor - ship. Let ev - 'ry na - tion bring

**Am7**        **Em**       **C**    **D**

from des - ert to the sea; all na - ture test - i - fies Your splen - dor.
to tell Your might-y deeds, to join the ev - er - last - ing chor - us.
its hon - ors to the King, a roar of har - mon - ies e - ter - nal.

**G**      **Am7**     **G/B**      **C**    **D**

Praise the Lord, praise the Lord, sing His great - ness, all cre - a - tion,

**Em**       **D/F♯**    **G/B**       **C**

praise the Lord, raise your voice, you heights and all you depths, from

Words and Music: Matt Boswell and Matt Papa

furth-est east to west, let ev - 'ry-thing that has breath praise the Lord!

west, you dis - tant burn-ing stars, all crea-tures near and far, from sky to sea to shore, sing out for ev - er - more, let ev - 'ry-thing that has breath praise the Lord!

# How Firm a Foundation

1. How firm a foun - da - tion, ye saints of the Lord,
2. "Fear not, I am with thee, O be not dis - mayed,
3. "When through fi - ery tri - als thy path - way shall lie,
4. "The soul that on Je - sus hath leaned for re - pose

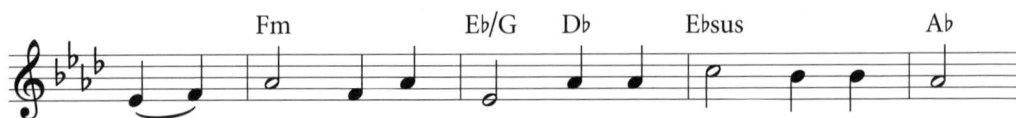

is laid for your faith in His ex - cel - lent Word!
for I am thy God— I will still give thee aid.
My grace, all - suf - fi - cient, shall be thy sup - ply;
I will not, I will not de - sert to his foes;

What more can He say than to you He has said,
I'll strength - en thee, help thee, and cause thee to stand,
the flame shall not hurt thee, I on - ly de - sign
that soul, though all hell should en - deav - or to shake,

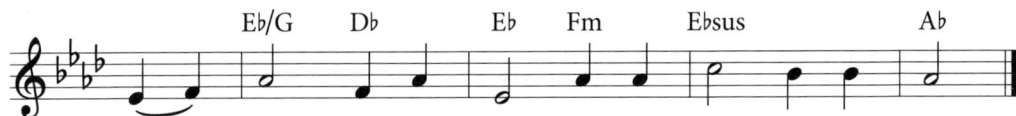

to you who for ref - uge to Je - sus have fled?
up - held by My right - eous, om - ni - po - tent hand."
thy dross to con - sume, and thy gold to re - fine."
I'll nev - er, no nev - er, no nev - er for - sake!"

Words: "K" in Rippon's *Selection*, 1787
Music: John Francis Wade, ca. 1743

FOUNDATION
11 11 11 11 with repeat

# O Lord, My Rock and My Redeemer

1. O Lord, my Rock and my Re-deem-er, great-est
2. O Lord, my Rock and my Re-deem-er, strong De -
3. O Lord, my Rock and my Re-deem-er, gra-cious

trea-sure of my long-ing soul, my God, like You there is no
fend-er of my wea-ry heart, my sword to fight the cruel de-
Sav-ior of my ru-ined life; my guilt and cross laid on Your

oth-er; true de-light is found in You a-lone. Your
ceiv-er, and my shield a-gainst his hate-ful darts. My
shoul-ders; in my place You suf-fered, bled, and died. You

grace, a well too deep to fath-om; Your love
song when en-e-mies sur-round me, my hope
rose— the grave and death are con-quered! You broke

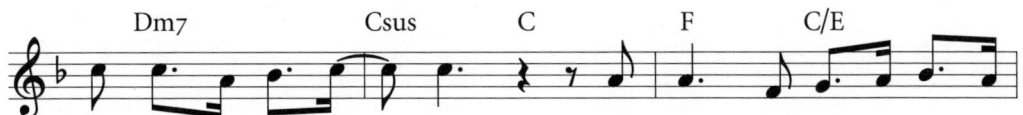

ex-ceeds the heav-ens' reach; Your truth, a fount of per-fect
when tides of sor-row rise, my joy when tri-als are a-
my bonds of sin and shame! O Lord, my Rock and my Re-

wis-dom, my high-est good, and my un-end-ing need.
bound-ing, Your faith-ful-ness, my ref-uge in the night.
deem-er, may all my days bring glo-ry to Your name.

Words and Music: Nathan Stiff © 2017 Sovereign Grace Worship

# Only a Holy God

1. Who else com-mands all the hosts of heav-en?
2. What oth-er beau - ty de - mands such prais - es?
3. What oth-er glo - ry con-sumes like fire?
4. Who else could res - cue me from my fail - ing?

Who else could make ev - 'ry king bow down?
What oth - er splen - dor out - shines the sun?
What oth - er pow - er can raise the dead?
Who else would of - fer His on - ly Son?

*1st time to v. 2*

Who else can whis-per and dark-ness trem-bles?
What oth-er maj - es - ty rules with jus - tice?
What oth-er name re-mains un - de - feat - ed?
Who else in - vites me to call Him Fa - ther?

On-ly a Ho-ly God.

Come and be-hold Him, the One and the On - ly. Cry out, sing ho - ly,

for - ev - er a Ho - ly God; come and wor-ship the Ho - ly God.

Words and Music: Jonny Robinson, Rich Thompson, Michael Farren, and Dustin Smith

# Great Is Thy Faithfulness

1. Great is Thy faith-ful-ness, O God my Fath-er; there is no
2. Sum-mer and win-ter, and spring-time and har-vest, sun, moon, and
3. Par-don for sin and a peace that en-dur-eth, Thine own dear

shad-ow of turn-ing with Thee; Thou chang-est not, Thy com -
stars in their cours-es a - bove join with all na - ture in
pres-ence to cheer and to guide; strength for to - day and bright

pas-sions, they fail not; as Thou hast been, Thou for - ev - er wilt be.
man - i - fold wit - ness to Thy great faith-ful-ness, mer - cy, and love.
hope for to - mor-row: bless-ings all mine, with ten thou-sand be - side!

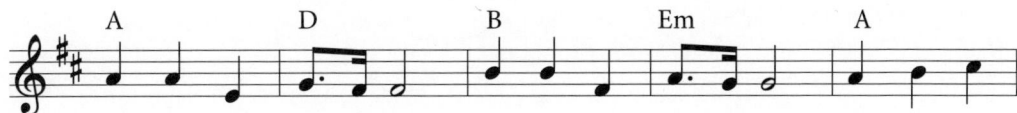

Great is Thy faith-ful-ness! Great is Thy faith-ful-ness! Morn-ing by

morn-ing new mer - cies I see; all I have need - ed Thy

hand hath pro - vid - ed: great is Thy faith-ful-ness, Lord, un - to me!

Words: Thomas O. Chisholm, 1923
Music: William M. Runyan, 1923

FAITHFULNESS
11 10 11 10 with refrain

# Taste and See (Psalm 34)

1. I sought the Lord, and He an-swered me, and de-liv-ered
2. This poor man cried and the Lord heard me, and saved me
3. O taste and see that the Lord is good. Oh, blessed is

me from ev-'ry fear. Those who look on Him are ra-di-
from my en-e-mies. The Son of God sur-rounds His
he who hides in Him. Oh fear the Lord, oh, all you

ant. They'll nev-er be a-shamed, they'll nev-er be a-
saints. He will de-liv-er them, He will de-liv-er
saints. He'll give you ev-'ry thing. He'll give you ev-'ry

shamed. them. Mag-ni-fy the Lord with me.
thing.

Come ex-alt His name to-geth - er. Glo-ri-fy the Lord

with me. Come ex-alt His name for-ev - er.

- er.

**Bridge**

Let us bless the Lord ev-'ry day and night. Nev-er

end-ing praise, may our in-cense rise. Let us bless the Lord ev-'ry

day and night. Nev-er end-ing praise, may our in-cense rise. Mag-ni-fy

the Lord with me. Come ex-alt His name to-geth-

- er, glo-ri-fy the Lord with me. Come ex-alt

His name for-ev - er. - er.

# Praise to the Lord, the Almighty

E    C#m    A    F#m7

1. Praise to the Lord, the Al - might - y, the King of cre -
2. Praise to the Lord, who o'er all things so won - drous - ly
3. Praise to the Lord, who with mar - vel - ous wis - dom has
4. Praise to the Lord, who doth pros - per thy work and de -
5. Praise to the Lord, oh let all that is in me a -

Bsus   B   E    E    C#m    A

a - tion; oh my soul, praise Him, for He is thy
reign - eth, shel - ters thee un - der His wings, yea, so
made thee, decked thee with health, and with lov - ing hand
fend thee; sure - ly His good - ness and mer - cy shall
dore Him! All that hath life and breath, come now with

F#m7    Bsus   B   E   E/G#    A    E

health and sal - va - tion. All ye who hear, now to His
gen - tly sus - tain - eth. Hast thou not seen how thy de -
guid - ed and stayed thee. How oft in grief has He not
dai - ly at - tend thee. Pon - der a - new what the Al -
prais - es be - fore Him! Let the A - men sound from His

A/C#    Bsus   B E/G#    C#m    B    E

tem - ple draw near: join me in glad ad - o - ra - tion!
si - res have been grant - ed in what He or - dain - eth?
brought thee re - lief, spread-ing His wings for to shade thee!
might - y can do, if with His love He be - friend thee.
peo - ple a - gain: glad - ly for - ev - er a - dore Him!

Words: Joachim Neander, 1680; trans. Catherine Winkworth, 1863, alt.
Music: *Ander Theil des Erneuerten Gesangbuchs*, Pt. 2, 1665     LOBE DEN HERREN

# All Hail the Power of Jesus' Name

G | Dsus | C | G

1. All hail the pow'r of Je - sus' name! Let an - gels pros - trate fall;
2. Ye cho - sen seed of Is - rael's race, ye ran - somed from the fall,
3. Let ev - 'ry kin - dred, ev - 'ry tribe on this ter - res - trial ball
4. O that with yon - der sa - cred throng we at His feet may fall!

G | Dsus | G | Em7 | Asus | D

bring forth the roy - al di - a - dem, and crown Him Lord of all!
hail Him who saves you by His grace, and crown Him Lord of all!
to Him all maj - es - ty as - cribe, and crown Him Lord of all!
We'll join the ev - er - last - ing song, and crown Him Lord of all!

G | Em | Dsus | G/B | C | Em | D | G

Bring forth the roy - al di - a - dem, and crown Him Lord of all!
Hail Him who saves you by His grace, and crown Him Lord of all!
To Him all maj - es - ty as - cribe, and crown Him Lord of all!
We'll join the ev - er - last - ing song, and crown Him Lord of all!

Words: Edward Perronet, 1779, and John Rippon, 1787
Music: Oliver Holden, 1793

CORONATION
86 86 86

# Is He Worthy?

1. Do you feel the world is bro - ken? *We do.* Do you
2. Is all cre - a - tion groan - ing? *It is.* Is a
3. Does the Fa - ther tru - ly love us? *He does.* Does the

feel the shad-ows deep - en? *We do.* But do you
new cre - a - tion com - ing? *It is.* Is the
Spir - it move a - mong us? *He does.* And does

know that all the dark won't stop the light from get-ting through? *We do.*
glo - ry of the Lord to be the light with - in our midst? *It is.*
Je - sus our Mes - si - ah hold for - ev - er those He loves? *He does.*

Do you wish that you could see it all made new? *We do.*
Is it good that we re - mind our-selves of this? *It is.*
Does our God in - tend to dwell a - gain with us? *He does.*

*1st time to v. 2*

Is an-y-one wor-thy? Is an-y-one whole? Is

an-y-one a - ble to break the seal and o - pen the scroll? The

Li-on of Ju - dah, who con-quered the grave; He is

Words and Music: Andrew Peterson and Ben Shive © 2018 Jakedog Music

Da-vid's Root and the Lamb who died to ran - som the slave. Is He

wor - thy? Is He wor - thy of all bless-ing and hon-or and glo - ry?

Is He wor-thy of this? He is. From ev-'ry

peo - ple and tribe, ev-'ry na-tion and tongue, He has

made us a king-dom and priests to God to reign with the Son. Is He

wor-thy? Is He wor - thy of all bless-ing and hon-or and glo - ry? Is He

wor-thy? Is He wor - thy? Is He wor - thy of this? He is!

Is He wor-thy? Is He wor-thy? He is! He is!

# In Christ Alone

1. In Christ a-lone my hope is found; He is my light, my strength, my
2. In Christ a-lone who took on flesh, full-ness of God in help-less
3. There in the ground His bod-y lay, Light of the world by dark-ness
4. No guilt in life, no fear in death: this is the pow'r of Christ in

song; this cor-ner-stone, this sol-id ground, firm through the
babe; this gift of love and right-eous-ness, scorned by the
slain. Then burst-ing forth in glo-rious day— up from the
me. From life's first cry to fi-nal breath, Je-sus com-

fierc-est drought and storm. What heights of love, what depths of
ones He came to save. Till on that cross as Je-sus
grave He rose a-gain! And as He stands in vic-to-
mands my des-ti-ny. No pow'r of hell, no scheme of

peace, when fears are stilled, when striv-ings cease! My com-for-
died, the wrath of God was sat-is-fied. For ev-'ry
ry, sin's curse has lost its grip on me. For I am
man can ev-er pluck me from His hand. Till He re-

ter, my all in all; here in the love of Christ I stand.
sin on Him was laid; here in the death of Christ I live.
His and He is mine, bought with the pre-cious blood of Christ.
turns or calls me home, here in the pow'r of Christ I'll stand.

Words and Music: Keith Getty and Stuart Townend © 2002 Thankyou Music

# All I Have Is Christ

1. I once was lost in dark-est night, yet thought I knew the way;
2. But as I ran my hell-bound race, in-dif-ferent to the cost,
3. Now Lord, I would be Yours a-lone, and live so all might see

the sin that prom-ised joy and life had led me to the grave.
You looked up-on my help-less state and led me to the cross.
the strength to fol-low Your com-mands could nev-er come from me.

I had no hope that You would own a re-bel to Your will,
And I be-held God's love dis-played: You suf-fered in my place.
O Fa-ther, use my ran-somed life in an-y way You choose,

and if You had not loved me first, I would re-fuse You
You bore the wrath re-served for me; now all I know is
and let my song for-ev-er be: "My on-ly boast is

still. grace. Hal-le-lu - jah, all I have is
You!"

Christ! Hal-le-lu - jah, Je-sus is my life!

Words and Music: Jordan Kauflin © 2008 Sovereign Grace Praise

# Christ the Sure and Steady Anchor

| D | | | Bm | A/C♯ | D |

1. Christ, the sure and stead-y an-chor, in the fu - ry of the storm;
2. Christ, the sure and stead-y an-chor, while the tem - pest rag-es on.
3. Christ, the sure and stead-y an-chor, through the floods of un - be - lief.
4. Christ, the sure and stead-y an-chor, as we face the waves of death.

| D | | A | A7 |

when the winds of doubt blow through me and my sails have all been torn.
When temp-ta - tion claims the bat - tle and it seems the night has won,
Hope-less some-how, O my soul, now lift your eyes to Cal - va - ry!
When these trials give way to glo - ry, as we draw our fi - nal breath,

| G | D | G | A | Bm |

In the suf - f'ring, in the sor - row, when my sink - ing hopes are few,
deep - er still then goes the an - chor, though I just - ly stand ac - cused.
This my bal - last of as - sur - ance, see His love for - ev - er proved.
we will cross that great ho - ri - zon, clouds be-hind and life se - cure.
*Tag: Christ, the shore of our sal - va - tion, ev - er faith - ful, ev - er true.*

*4th time repeat italics*

| D | Bm | A | D |

I will hold fast to the an - chor— it shall nev - er be re - moved.
I will hold fast to the an - chor— it shall nev - er be re - moved.
I will hold fast to the an - chor— it shall nev - er be re - moved.
And the calm will be the bet - ter, for the storms that we en - dure.
*We will hold fast to the an - chor— it shall nev - er be re - moved.*

Words and Music: Matt Boswell and Matt Papa © 2014 Doxology and Theology, Love Your Enemies Publishing

# Blessed Assurance

1. Bless-ed as - sur - ance: Je - sus is mine! Oh, what a fore - taste of
2. Per - fect sub - mis - sion, per-fect de - light, vi - sions of rap - ture now
3. Per - fect sub - mis - sion: all is at rest, I in my Sav - ior am

glo - ry di - vine! Heir of sal - va - tion, pur - chase of God,
burst on my sight; an - gels de - scend - ing, bring from a - bove
hap - py and blest; watch-ing and wait - ing, look - ing a - bove,

born of His Spir - it, washed in His blood.
ech - oes of mer - cy, whis - pers of love. This is my sto - ry,
filled with His good - ness, lost in His love.

this is my song, prais-ing my Sav - ior all the day long; this is my

sto - ry, this is my song, prais-ing my Sav - ior all the day long.

Words: Fanny Crosby, 1873
Music: Phoebe P. Knapp, 1873

ASSURANCE

# Yet Not I but Through Christ in Me

**C**      **F**

1. What gift of grace is Je-sus, my Re-deem-er; there is no
2. The night is dark, but I am not for-sak-en, for by my
3. No fate I dread; I know I am for-giv-en; the fu-ture
4. With ev-'ry breath I long to fol-low Je-sus, for He has

**C**      **Am**    **G**      **C**

more for heav-en now to give. He is my joy, my right-eous-ness and
side, the Sav-ior, He will stay. I la-bor on in weak-ness and re-
sure, the price, it has been paid. For Je-sus bled and suf-fered for my
said that He will bring me home. And day by day I know He will re-

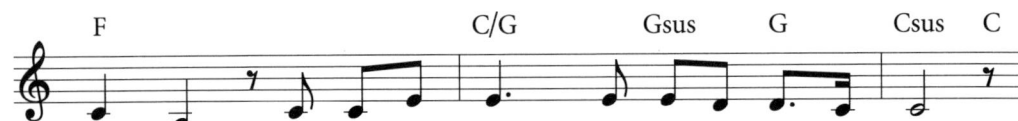

**F**      **C/G**    **Gsus**    **G**      **Csus**    **C**

free-dom, my stead-fast love, my deep and bound-less peace.
joic-ing, for in my need His pow-er is dis-played.
par-don, and He was raised to o-ver-throw the grave.
new me un-til I stand with joy be-fore the throne.

**/E**    **F**      **C**      **F**

To this I hold: my hope is on-ly Je-sus, for my life is
To this I hold: my Shep-herd will de-fend me; through the deep-est
To this I hold: my sin has been de-feat-ed; Je-sus now and
To this I hold: my hope is on-ly Je-sus; all the glo-ry

**C/E**      **Gsus**    **G**      **C**      **Dm7**

whol-ly bound to His. Oh, how strange and di-vine, I can
val-ley He will lead. Oh, the night has been won, and I
ev-er is my plea. Oh, the chains are re-leased, I can
ev-er-more to Him. When the race is com-plete, still my

Words and Music: Jonny Robinson, Rich Thompson, and Michael Farren © 2018 CityAlight Music

| sing: | all | is | mine! | Yet | not | I, | but through Christ | in | me. |
| shall | o - ver - come! | Yet | not | I, | but through Christ | in | me. |
| sing: | "I | am | free!" | Yet | not | I, | but through Christ | in | me. |
| lips | shall re - peat: | "Yet | not | I, | but through Christ | in | me." |

# Turn Your Eyes

1. Turn your eyes up-on Je - sus, look full in His won-der-ful face.
2. Turn your eyes to the hill - side where jus-tice and mer-cy em - brace.
3. Turn your eyes to the morn - ing and see Christ the li - on a - wake.
4. Turn your eyes to the heav - ens, our King will re - turn for His own.

And the things of earth will grow strange - ly dim in the light of His
There the Son of God gave His life for us, and our meas-ure - less
What a glo-rious dawn: fear of death is gone, for we car - ry His
Ev - 'ry knee will bow, ev - 'ry tongue will shout, "All the glo - ry to

glo - ry and grace. *to v. 2*
debt was e - rased.
life in our veins.
Je - sus a - lone!"

Je - sus, to You we lift our eyes,

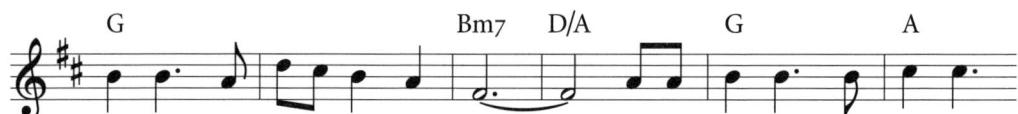

Je - sus, our glo - ry and our prize. We a - dore You, be - hold You,

our Sav-ior ev - er true. Oh Je - sus, we turn our eyes to You.

Words and Music: Helen H. Lemmel
Additional words and chorus by George Romanacce, Nic Trout, Kevin Winebarger, and Nathan Stiff

# Christ Our Wisdom

Bb          Eb

1. Christ our wis-dom, we are hum-bled when You hide Your ways from
2. Christ our wis-dom, be our glad-ness when we fail to un-der-
3. Christ our wis-dom, we will fol-low though the way a-head is
4. Christ our wis-dom, we a-dore You for the beau-ty of the

Bb

us; You have pur-pos-es un-num-bered, each one
stand; You or-dain all joy and sad-ness to ful-
veiled; as we jour-ney through the shad-ows, grant us
cross; once in fool-ish-ness we scorned You, but Your

F7sus          Bb          Eb

good and glo-ri-ous. Help us trust when we grow
fill Your per-fect plan. Help us know You rule with
faith where sight has failed. Help us cling to Your com-
blood has ran-somed us. Help us sing the end-less

F          Gm          Eb

wea-ry, free us from our anx-ious thoughts; give us
pow-er o-ver ev-'ry rag-ing flood; in our
mand-ments, strength-ened by Your faith-ful Word; we will
mer-cies of Your hum-ble heart to save; Christ our

Bb/D          Eb          F7sus          Bb

grace to see more clear-ly; You are God, and we are not.
most un-cer-tain hour, You are God, and we are loved.
nev-er be a-ban-doned; You are God, and we are Yours.
wis-dom, Christ our glo-ry, You are God, for-ev-er praised.

Words and Music: Jon Althoff, Bob Kauflin, and Nathan Stiff © 2024 Sovereign Grace Praise

# The Solid Rock

1. My hope is built on noth-ing less than Je-sus' blood and
2. When dark-ness seems to hide His face, I rest on His un -
3. His oath, His cov - e - nant, His blood sup - port me in the
4. When He shall come with trum - pet sound, oh, may I then in

right - eous - ness; I dare not trust the sweet - est frame, but
chang - ing grace; in ev - 'ry high and storm - y gale, my
whelm - ing flood; when all a - round my soul gives way, He
Him be found, dressed in His right - eous - ness a - lone, fault -

whol - ly lean on Je - sus' name.
an - chor holds with - in the veil. On Christ, the sol - id Rock, I stand;
then is all my hope and stay.
less to stand be - fore the throne.

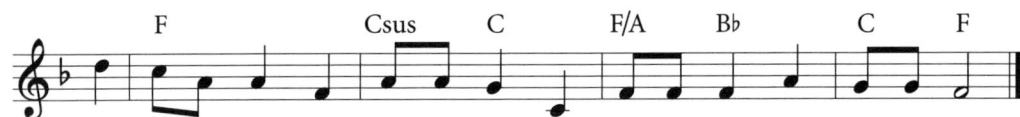

all oth - er ground is sink - ing sand; all oth - er ground is sink - ing sand.

Words: Edward Mote, 1824; alt. John Rees, 1826
Music: William Bradbury, 1864

# Jesus, Strong and Kind

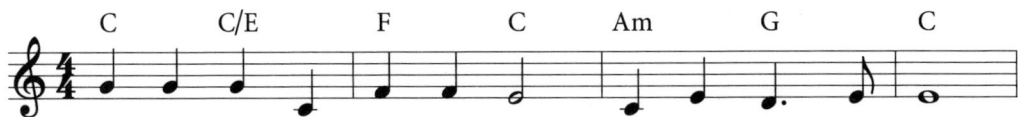

| C | C/E | F | C | Am | G | C |
|---|---|---|---|---|---|---|

1. Je - sus said that if I thirst, I should come to Him.
2. Je - sus said if I am weak, I should come to Him.
3. Je - sus said that if I fear, I should come to Him.
4. Je - sus said if I am lost, He will come to me.

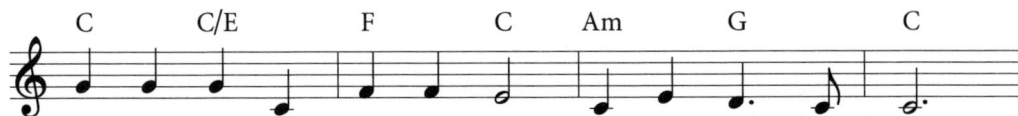

| C | C/E | F | C | Am | G | C |
|---|---|---|---|---|---|---|

No one else can sat - is - fy; I should come to Him. *to v. 2*
No one else can be my strength; I should come to Him.
No one else can be my shield; I should come to Him.
And He showed me on that cross He will come to me.

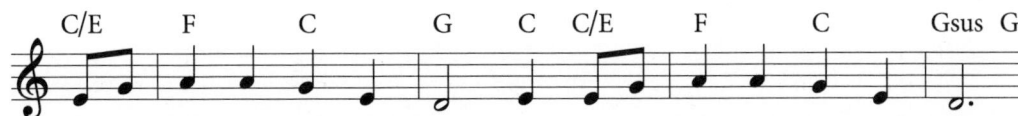

| C/E | F | C | G | C | C/E | F | C | Gsus G |
|---|---|---|---|---|---|---|---|---|

For the Lord is good and faith - ful; He will keep us day and night.

| C/E | F | C | G | Am | F | G | C |
|---|---|---|---|---|---|---|---|

We can al - ways run to Je - sus: Je - sus, strong and kind.

Words and Music: Colin Buchanan, Jonny Robinson, Michael Farren, and Rich Thompson
© 2019 CityAlight Music, Farren Love And War Publishing, Integrity's Alleluia! Music, Wanaaring Road Music

# Show Us Christ

1. Pre-pare our hearts, O God, help us to re-ceive.
2. Your Word is liv-ing light up-on our dark-ened eyes,

Break the hard and ston-y ground, help our un-be-lief.
guards us through temp-ta-tions, makes the sim-ple wise. Your

Plant Your Word down deep in us, cause it to bear fruit,
Word is food for fam-ished ones, free-dom for the slave,

*Chorus*

o-pen up our ears to hear, lead us in Your truth. Show us Christ,
rich-es for the need-y soul, come speak to us to-day.

show us Christ, O God, re-veal Your glo-

-ry through the preach-ing of Your Word un-til ev-'ry heart

Words: Doug Plank; Music: Doug Plank and Bob Kauflin
© 2011 Sovereign Grace Worship

con - fess - es   Christ   is   Lord.   Where else can we go,   Lord,

*to Chorus, sung twice*

where else can we go?   You have the words of e - ter - nal life.

# It Was Finished upon That Cross

1. How I love the voice of Je-sus on the cross of Cal-va-ry.
2. Now the curse, it has been bro-ken, Je-sus paid the price for me.

He de-clares His work is fin-ished, He has spok-en this hope to me.
Full, the par-don He has of-fered. Great, the wel-come that I re-ceive.

Though the sun had ceased its shin-ing though the war ap-peared as lost.
Bold-ly I ap-proach my Fa-ther, clothed in Je-sus' right-eous-ness.

Christ has tri-umphed o-ver e-vil, it was fin-ished up-on that cross.
There is no more guilt to car-ry, it was fin-ished up-on that cross.

3. Death was once my great op-pon-ent, fear once had a hold on me.

Words and Music: Jonny Robinson, Rich Thompson, and Nigel Hendroff
© 2021 CityAlight Music

But the Son who died to save us rose that we would be

free in - deed! Yes, He rose that we would be free in - deed!

Free from ev - 'ry plan of dark - ness, free to live and free to love.
On - ward to e - ter - nal glo - ry, to my Sav - ior and my God.

Death is dead and Christ is ris - en, it was fin - ished up -
I re - joice in Je - sus' vic - t'ry, it was fin - ished up -

1.
on that cross. 2. - on that cross. It was fin - ished up - on that cross.

It was fin - ished up - on that cross.

# I Stand Amazed (My Savior's Love)

*(G) ... (G/B) (D)*

1. I stand a - mazed in the pre - sence of Je - sus, the
2. For me it was in the gar - den He prayed, "Not My
3. In pit - y an - gels be - held Him, and came from the
4. He took my sins and my sor - rows; He made them His
5. When with the ran - somed in glo - ry His face I at

*(G) ... (C) ... (G) (G/B) (C)*

Naz - a - rene, and won - der how He could love me, a
will, but Thine." He had no tears for His own griefs, but
world of light to com - fort Him in the sor - rows He
ver - y own. He bore the bur - den to Cal - v'ry, and
last shall see, 'twill be my joy through the a - ges to

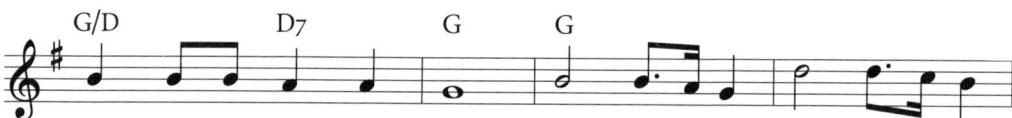

*(G/D) (D7) (G) (G)*

sin - ner con-demned, un - clean.
sweat drops of blood for mine.
bore for my soul that night. How mar-vel-ous! How won-der-ful!
suf - fered and died a - lone.
sing of His love for me.

*(D) ... (G/D) (D7) (G/D) (D) (G)*

And my song shall ev - er be: How mar - vel - ous!

*(C) (G/D) (Dsus) (G)*

How won - der - ful is my Sav - ior's love for me!

Words and Music: Charles Gabriel, 1905

# Grace Greater Than Our Sin

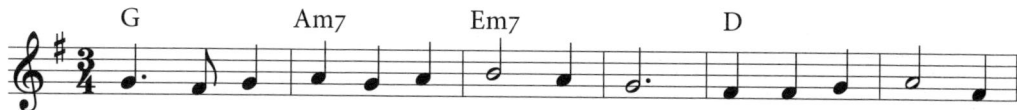

**G · Am7 · Em7 · D**

1. Mar - vel - ous grace of our lov - ing Lord, grace that ex - ceeds our
2. Sin and de - spair, like the sea waves cold threat - en the soul with
3. Dark is the stain that we can - not hide— what can a - vail to
4. Mar - vel - ous, in - fi - nite, match - less grace, free - ly be - stowed on

**C/E · D/F♯ · G · Em · Dsus · G · Em**

sin and our guilt; yon - der on Cal - va - ry's mount out - poured,
in - fi - nite loss; grace that is great - er, yes, grace un - told,
wash it a - way? Look! there is flow - ing a crim - son tide;
all who be - lieve; you that are long - ing to see His face,

**Am/C · Am · Dsus · G · G**

there where the blood of the Lamb was spilled.
points to the ref - uge, the might - y cross. Grace, grace,
whit - er than snow you may be to - day.
will you this mo - ment His grace re - ceive?

**C/G · G · Dsus · D · C · G**

God's grace; grace that will par - don and cleanse with - in!

**G · C/G · G · Am/C · Am · Dsus · G**

Grace, grace, God's grace; grace that is great - er than all our sin!

Words: Julia Johnston, 1910
Music: Daniel Towner, 1910

MOODY

# Come Behold the Wondrous Mystery

*D · G · D · A*

1. Come, be - hold the won-drous mys-t'ry, in the dawn-ing of the King.
2. Come, be - hold the won-drous mys-t'ry, He the per - fect Son of Man.
3. Come, be - hold the won-drous mys-t'ry, Christ the Lord up - on the tree.
4. Come, be - hold the won-drous mys-t'ry, slain by death the God of life.

*Bm7 · G · D/F♯ · Em7 · Asus · D*

He, the theme of heav-en's prais - es, robed in frail hu - man - i - ty.
In His liv - ing, in His suf - f'ring, nev - er trace nor stain of sin.
In the stead of ru - ined sin - ners hangs the Lamb in vic - to - ry.
But no grave could e'er re - strain Him; praise the Lord; He is a - live!

*G · F♯m · Bm · G*

In our long - ing, in our dark - ness, now the light of life has come!
See the true and bet - ter Ad - am, come to save the hell-bound man.
See the price of our re - demp - tion, see the Fa - ther's plan un - fold.
What a fore - taste of de - liv - 'rance, how un - wa - ver - ing our hope.

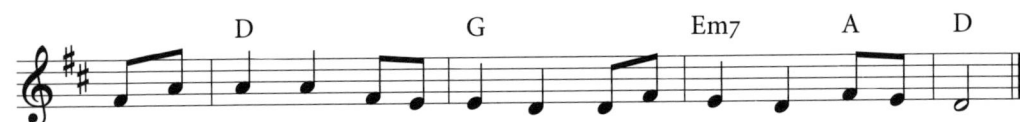

*D · G · Em7 · A · D*

Look to Christ who con - de - scend - ed, took on flesh to ran - som us.
Christ, the great and sure ful - fill - ment of the law; in Him we stand.
Bring - ing man - y sons to glo - ry, grace un - meas - ured, love un - told.
Christ in pow - er res - ur - rect - ed as we will be when He comes.

# Fairest Lord Jesus

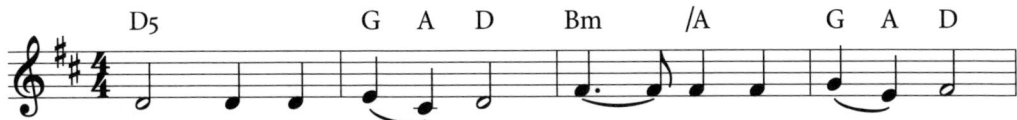

D5 · · · · · G · A · D · · Bm · /A · · G · A · D

1. Fair - est Lord Je - sus, Ru - ler of all na - ture,
2. Fair are the mead - ows, fair - er still the wood - lands,
3. Fair is the sun - shine, fair - er still the moon - light,
4. Beau - ti - ful Sav - ior! Lord of the na - tions!

D · G · D · Dsus · D · A/C# · D · A · D/F# · · · Bsus · B · Em

O Thou of God and man the Son, Thee will I cher - ish,
robed in the bloom - ing garb of spring: Je - sus is fair - er,
and all the twink - ling star - ry host: Je - sus shines bright - er,
Son of God and Son of Man! Glo - ry and hon - or,

Em · · · Asus · A · D · · Bm · · G · · D/A · A7 · · D

Thee will I hon - or, Thou, my soul's glo - ry, joy, and crown!
Je - sus is pur - er, who makes the woe - ful heart to sing.
Je - sus shines pur - er, than all the an - gels heav'n can boast.
praise, ad - o - ra - tion, now and for - ev - er - more be Thine!

Words: *Münsterisch Gesangbuch*, 1677; trans. *Evangelical Christendom* (st. 1–3), 1850,
 and J.A. Seiss (st. 4), 1873
Music: Silesian folk melody, *Schlesische Volkslieder*, 1842

CRUSADERS' HYMN
56 85 58

# All Sufficient Merit

| | F#m | E | D | A/C# | D | E |
|---|---|---|---|---|---|---|
| 1. | All-suf-fi-cient mer - it | | | shin-ing like the sun, |
| 2. | In love He con-de-scend-ed, | | | e-ter-nal now in time. |
| 3. | I lay down my gar - ments, | | | an-y emp-ty boasts. |
| 4. | All-suf-fi-cient mer - it, | | | firm in life and death. |

| F#m | E | D | A/C# | D | E | Asus | A |
|---|---|---|---|---|---|---|---|

a for-tune I in-her - it, by no work I have done.
A life with-out a blem - ish, the Mak-er made to die.
Good works now all cor-rupt-ed by the sin-ful host.
The joy of my sal-va - tion shall be my fi-nal breath.

**E F#m D A**

My right-eous-ness I for - feit at my Sav-ior's cross,
The law could nev-er save us, our law-less-ness had won,
I'm dressed in my Lord Je - sus, a crim-son robe made white.
When I stand ac-cept-ed be-fore the throne of God,

**E F#m D E A**

where all-suf-fi-cient mer - it did what I could not. *to v.2*
un-til the pure and spot-less Lamb had fin-ally come.
No more fear of judg - ment, His right-eous-ness is mine.
I'll gaze up-on my Je - sus and thank Him for the cross.

**E F#m C#m D A**

It is done, it is fin-ished, no more debt I owe.

**E F#m C#m D E A**

Paid in full, all-suf-fi-cient mer - it now my own.

Words and Music: Bethany Barnard, Shane Barnard, and Bryan Fowler
© 2023 More Songs from Wellhouse

# There Is One Gospel

1. There is one gos - pel on which I stand for all e - ter - ni - ty.
2. There is one gos - pel to which I cling, all else I count as loss.
3. There is one gos - pel where hope is found, the emp - ty tomb still speaks.
4. And in this gos - pel, the Church is one, we do not walk a - lone.

It is my sto - ry, my Fa - ther's plan, the Son has res - cued me.
For there, where jus - tice and mer - cy meet, He saved me on the cross.
For death could not keep my Sav - ior down, He lives and I am free.
We have His Spir - it as we press on to lead us safe - ly home.

Oh, what a gos - pel, oh what a peace. My high - est joy and my
No more I boast in what I can bring, no more I car - ry the
Now on my Sav - ior I fix my eyes, my life is His and His
And when in glo - ry still I will sing of this old sto - ry that

deep - est need. Now and for - ev - er, He is my light.
weight of sin. For He has brought me from death to life.
hope is mine. For He has prom - ised I, too, will rise.
res - cued me. Praise to my Sav - ior, the King of life.

I stand in the gos - pel of Je - sus Christ.

Words and Music: Jonny Robinson and Rich Thompson © 2022 CityAlight Music

# When I Survey the Wondrous Cross

1. When I sur-vey the won-drous cross on which the
2. For-bid it, Lord, that I should boast, save in the
3. See from His head, His hands, His feet, sor-row and
4. Were the whole realm of na-ture mine, that were a

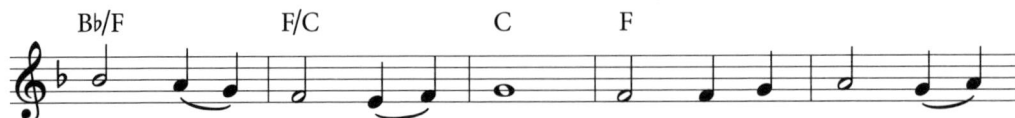

Prince of Glo-ry died, my rich-est gain I
death of Christ, my God! All the vain things that
love flow min-gled down! Did e'er such love and
pre-sent far too small; love so a-maz-ing,

count but loss, and pour con-tempt on all my pride.
charm me most, I sac-ri-fice them to His blood.
sor-row meet, or thorns com-pose so rich a crown?
so di-vine, de-mands my soul, my life, my all.

Words: Isaac Watts, 1707
Music: Lowell Mason, 1825

HAMBURG
LM

# The Power of the Cross

F/A  G/B  C  C  G7sus/D  C/E  F

1. Oh, to see the dawn  of the dark - est day—  Christ on the
2. Oh, to see the pain  writ - ten on Your face,  bear - ing the
3. Now the day - light flees;  now the ground be - neath  quakes as its
4. Oh, to see my name  writ - ten in the wounds,  for through Your

C/E  Dm7  Fmaj7  Gsus  G  F/A  G/B  C  C

road to Cal - va - ry.  Tried by sin - ful men,  torn and
awe - some weight of sin;  ev - 'ry bit - ter thought,  ev - 'ry
Ma - ker bows His head.  Cur - tain torn in two,  dead are
suf - f'ring I am free.  Death is crushed to death,  life is

G7sus/D  C/E  F  C/E  Fmaj7  Gsus  G  C/E

beat - en, then  nailed to a cross of wood.
e - vil deed  crown - ing Your blood - stained brow.  1–3. This the
raised to life,  "Fin - ished!" the vic - t'ry cry!  4. This the
mine to live,  won through Your self - less love!

F  G/B  C  C/E  F  G/B  C

pow'r of the cross:  Christ be - came sin for us.
pow'r of the cross:  Son of God— slain for us.

C/E  F  D/F#  G  G/F  C/E  F  Gsus  G  C

Took the blame,  bore the wrath—we stand for - giv - en at the cross!
What a love!  What a cost! We stand for - giv - en at the cross!

Words and Music: Stuart Townend and Keith Getty © 2005 Thankyou Music

# Christ Is Mine Forevermore

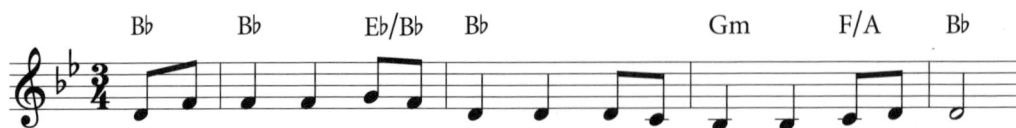

1. Mine are days that God has num-bered; I was made to walk with Him.
2. Mine are tears in times of sor - row, dark-ness not yet un - der-stood.
3. Mine are days here as a stran - ger, pil-grim on a nar-row way.

Yet I look for world-ly trea - sure and for - sake the King of kings.
Thru the val - ley I must trav - el where I see no earth-ly good.
One with Christ I will en - coun - ter harm and ha - tred for His name.

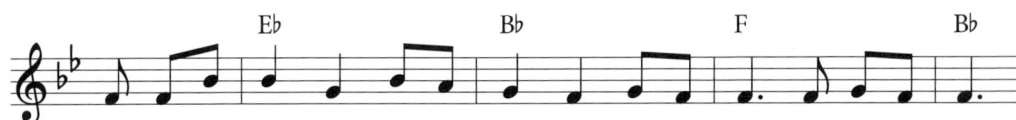

But mine is hope in my Re - deem-er; though I fall, His love is sure.
But mine is peace that flows from heav - en, and the strength in times of need.
But mine is ar - mor for this bat - tle, strong e - nough to last the war.
*Tag: And mine are keys to Zi - on's ci - ty where be - side the King I walk.*

*last time to Bridge*

For Christ has paid for eve - ry fail - ing; I am His for - ev - er-more.
I know my pain will not be wast - ed; Christ com-pletes His work in me.
And He has said He will de - liv - er safe - ly to the gold-en shore.
*For there my heart has found its trea - sure: Christ is mine for - ev - er-more.*

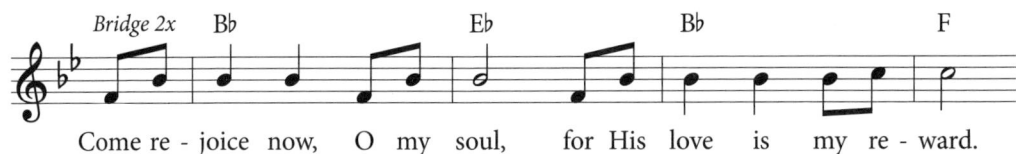

*Bridge 2x*

Come re - joice now, O my soul, for His love is my re - ward.

*2nd time to Tag*

Fear is gone and hope is sure; Christ is mine for - ev - er - more.

Words and Music: Jonny Robinson and Rich Thompson © 2016 CityAlight Music

# He Will Hold Me Fast

1. When I fear my faith will fail, Christ will hold me fast;
2. Those He saves are His de - light; Christ will hold me fast;
3. For my life He bled and died— Christ will hold me fast;

when the tempt - er would pre - vail, He will hold me fast.
pre - cious in His ho - ly sight, He will hold me fast.
jus - tice has been sat - is - fied; He will hold me fast.

I could nev - er keep my hold through life's fear - ful path;
He'll not let my soul be lost; His prom - is - es shall last;
Raised with Him to end - less life— He will hold me fast,

for my love is of - ten cold: He must hold me fast.
bought by Him at such a cost, He will hold me fast.
till our faith is turned to sight when He comes at last!

He will hold me fast; He will hold me fast;

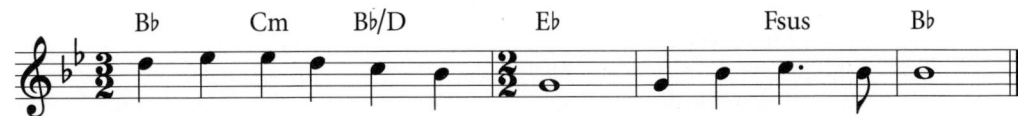

for my Sav - ior loves me so— He will hold me fast.

Words: Ada Habershon, 1906; additional lyrics by Matt Merker
Music: Matt Merker
© 2016 Getty Music Songs and Matt Merker

# Jesus, I My Cross Have Taken

**E**     **G#m**     **A**     **E**

1. Je - sus, I my cross have tak - en,
2. Let the world de - spise and leave me,
3. Man may trou - ble and dis - tress me;
4. Go, then, earth - ly fame and treas - ure;
5. Soul, then know thy full sal - va - tion,
6. Haste thee on from grace to glo - ry,

**G#m**     **A**     **B**

all to leave and fol - low Thee;
they have left my Sav - ior too.
'twill but drive me to Thy breast.
come dis - as - ter, scorn, and pain;
rise o'er sin and fear and care;
armed by faith, and winged by pray'r.

**E**     **G#m**     **A**     **E**

des - ti - tute, de - spised, for - sak - en,
Hu - man hearts and looks de - ceive me,
Life with tri - als hard may press me;
in Thy ser - vice, pain is pleas - ure;
joy to find in ev - 'ry sta - tion,
Heav'n's e - ter - nal days be - fore thee;

**G#m**     **A**     **E**

Thou from hence my all shalt be.
Thou art not like them un - true.
heav'n will bring me sweet - er rest.
with Thy fa - vor, loss is gain.
some - thing still to do or bear.
God's own hand shall guide us there.

Words: Henry Lyte, 1824
Music: Bill Moore © 2001 Bill Moore Music

**C#m**        **C#m/B**        **A**        **E**

| | | | | | | | |
|---|---|---|---|---|---|---|---|
| Per - | ish | ev - | 'ry | fond | am - | bi - | tion, |
| Oh, | while | Thou | dost | smile | up - | on | me, |
| Oh, | 'tis | not | in | grief | to | harm | me |
| I | have called | Thee | Ab - | ba, | Fa - | ther; | |
| Think what | Spir - | it | dwells | with - | in | thee; | |
| Soon | shall | close | thy | earth - | ly | mis - | sion, |

**C#m**        **C#m/B**        **A**        **E**

| | | | | | | |
|---|---|---|---|---|---|---|
| all | I've | sought | or | hoped | or | known, |
| God | of | wis - | dom, | love | and | might, |
| while | Thy | love | is | left | to | me; |
| I | have stayed | my | heart | on | Thee; | |
| think what | Fa - | ther's | smiles | are | thine; | |
| soon | shall | pass | thy | pil - | grim | days; |

**C#m**        **C#m/B**        **A**        **E**

| | | | | | | | |
|---|---|---|---|---|---|---|---|
| yet | how | rich | is | my | con - | di - | tion: |
| foes | may | hate | and | friends | dis - | own | me: |
| oh, | 'twere | not | in | joy | to | charm | me, |
| think | that | Je - | sus | died | to | win | thee— |
| hope | shall | change | to | glad | fru - | i - | tion, |

**F#m**   **E/G#**     **A**        **B**        **E**

| | | | | | | |
|---|---|---|---|---|---|---|
| God | and | heav'n | are | still | my | own. |
| show | Thy | face | and | all | is | bright. |
| were | that | joy | un - mixed | with | | Thee. |
| all | must | work | for | good | to | me. |
| child | of | heav'n, | canst | thou | re - | pine? |
| faith | to | sight | and | pray'r | to | praise. |

# Be Thou My Vision

1. Be Thou my Vi-sion, O Lord of my heart; naught be all
2. Be Thou my Wis-dom and Thou my true Word; I ev-er
3. Rich-es I heed not, nor man's emp-ty praise, Thou mine in-
4. High King of heav-en, my vic-to-ry won, may I reach

else to me, save that Thou art— Thou my best thought, by
with Thee and Thou with me, Lord; Thou my great Fa - ther,
her - i - tance, now and al - ways; Thou and Thou on - ly,
heav-en's joys, bright heav-en's Sun! Heart of my own heart, what-

day or by night, wak - ing or sleep-ing, Thy pres-ence my light.
I Thy true son, Thou in me dwell-ing, and I with Thee one.
first in my heart, High King of heav - en, my trea-sure Thou art.
ev - er be - fall, still be my Vi - sion, O Rul - er of all.

Words: Irish hymn, 10th cent.; trans. Mary Elizabeth Byrne, 1905; vers. Eleanor Hull, 1912

SLANE
10 10 10 10

Music: Irish folk melody

# Dear Refuge of My Weary Soul

1. Dear Ref - uge of my wea - ry soul, on Thee, when sor - rows rise,
2. But oh! When gloom - y doubts pre - vail, I fear to call Thee mine;
3. Hast Thou not bid me seek Thy face, and shall I seek in vain?
4. Thy mer - cy seat is o - pen still, here let my soul re - treat;

on Thee, when waves of trou - ble roll, my faint - ing hope re - lies.
the springs of com - fort seem to fail, and all my hopes de - cline.
And can the ear of sov - 'reign grace be deaf when I com - plain?
with hum - ble hope at - tend Thy will, and wait be - neath Thy feet.

To Thee I tell each ris - ing grief, for Thou a - lone can heal;
Yet gra - cious God, where shall I flee? Thou art my on - ly trust;
No, still the ear of sov - 'reign grace at - tends the mourn - er's prayer;
Thy mer - cy seat is o - pen still, here let my soul re - treat;

Thy word can bring a sweet re - lief for ev - 'ry pain I feel.
and still my soul would cleave to Thee, though pros - trate in the dust.
O may I ev - er find ac - cess to breathe my sor - rows there.
with hum - ble hope at - tend Thy will, and wait be - neath Thy feet.

Words: Anne Steele, 1760
Music: Matt Merker © 2014 Matthew Merker Music / Sovereign Grace Praise

# Speak O Lord

1. Speak, O Lord, as we come to You to re - ceive the food of Your ho - ly Word. Take Your truth, plant it deep in us; shape and fash - ion us in Your like - ness; that the light of Christ might be seen to-day in our acts of love and our deeds of faith. Speak, O Lord, and ful - fill in us all Your pur - pos - es for Your glo - ry.

2. Teach us, Lord, full o - be - di - ence, ho - ly rev - er - ence, true hu - mil - i - ty; test our thoughts and our at - ti - tudes in the ra - di - ance of Your pu - ri - ty. Cause our faith to rise; cause our eyes to see Your ma - jes - tic love and au - thor - i - ty. Words of pow'r that can nev - er fail: let their truth pre-vail o - ver un - be - lief.

3. Speak, O Lord, and re - new our minds; help us grasp the heights of Your plans for us: truths un - changed from the dawn of time that will ech - o down through e - ter - ni - ty. And by grace we'll stand on Your prom - is - es, and by faith we'll walk as You walk with us. Speak, O Lord, till Your church is built and the earth is filled with Your glo - ry.

# All of Our Tomorrows

1. This spin-ning world by Your own hand hurls ev - er on a -
2. May zeal-ous youth and cau - tious age de - ter - mine not the
3. When win - ter makes us rem - i - nisce of warm - er days so
4. Hands to the plow, we're press-ing on, and run - ning hard to

round the sun. The sea - sons march at Your com-mand; the
steps we choose; Great Shep-herd, guide us through each day, oh,
dis - tant now, of cher-ished saints the sun once kissed whose
win the prize, em - pow-ered by the love of God with

old de - parts, the new year comes. And though ce - les - tial is Your
how we want to fol - low You. Come, Liv - ing Way, our way make
beau - ty passed be - hind the clouds, let all our fond and long-ing
grace be - fore and grace be - hind. For lo, what hope be - fore us

gaze, You search and care for all our ways; we of - fer up to
clear; let per - fect love drive out our fear; be Thou our vi - sion,
tears re - mind us we are pil-grims here; we trust You, Sov-ereign
stands: You fin - ish all that You be - gan; e - ter - nal joy is

You this day and all of our to - mor - rows.
now and here and all of our to - mor - rows.
of our years, with all of our to - mor - rows.
in Your hands, and all of our to - mor - rows.

Words and Music: Dave Fournier and Ryan Foglesong © 2020 Sovereign Grace Worship

# By Faith

1. By faith we see the hand of God in the light of cre-
2. By faith our fa-thers roamed the earth, with the pow'r of His
3. By faith the proph-ets saw a day when the longed-for Mes-
4. By faith the church was called to go in the pow'r of the
5. By faith this moun-tain shall be moved, and the pow'r of the

a-tion's grand de-sign, in the lives of those who prove His
prom-ise in their hearts of a ho-ly cit-y built by
si-ah would ap-pear, with the pow'r to break the chains of
Spir-it to the lost, to de-liv-er cap-tives and to
gos-pel shall pre-vail; for we know in Christ all things are

faith-ful-ness, who walk by faith and not by sight.
God's own hand, a place where peace and jus-tice reign.
sin and death and rise tri-um-phant from the grave.
preach good news in ev-'ry cor-ner of the earth.
pos-si-ble for all who call up-on His name.

We will stand as chil-dren of the prom-ise; we will

fix our eyes on Him, our soul's re-ward; till the race is fin-ished

and the work is done, we'll walk by faith and not by sight.

Words and Music: Stuart Townend, Keith Getty, and Kristyn Getty © 2009 Thankyou Music

# Be Still, Be Still My Soul (Psalm 46)

F    Am    C    Fmaj7

1. Should moun-tains melt in - to the roar - ing o - ceans,
2. When all I see are en - e - mies be - fore me,
3. Though all a - round the wick - ed seem to pros - per,
4. Though wars e - rupt, You will not leave us or - phans,

Am    C    Fmaj7

the earth give way, or heav-en's lights grow cold, O might - y
when un - be - lief and doubt have tak - en hold, O Lord of
they mock Your name and rise a - gainst Your throne, O right-eous
though na - tions rage, You guard us as Your own. O, Prince of

Am    C    Fmaj7    C/E  F    G    C

God, You are my strong De-fend - er; be still, be still, my soul.
hosts, You prom - ise to de - feat them; be still, be still, my soul.
Judge, their deeds You will re - mem - ber; be still, be still, my soul.
Peace, we will not be a - ban-doned; be still, be still, my soul.

F    Am    C    F    Am    G

For You are God, I need not fear, You're sov-'reign o - ver all. For

F    Am    C    F    Am    G    C

You are good and al-ways near, I'll rest in You a - lone, be still, my soul.

Words and Music: Ryan Foglesong, Grace Nixon, and Nathan Stiff © 2022 Sovereign Grace Praise

# Surely Goodness, Surely Mercy (Psalm 23)

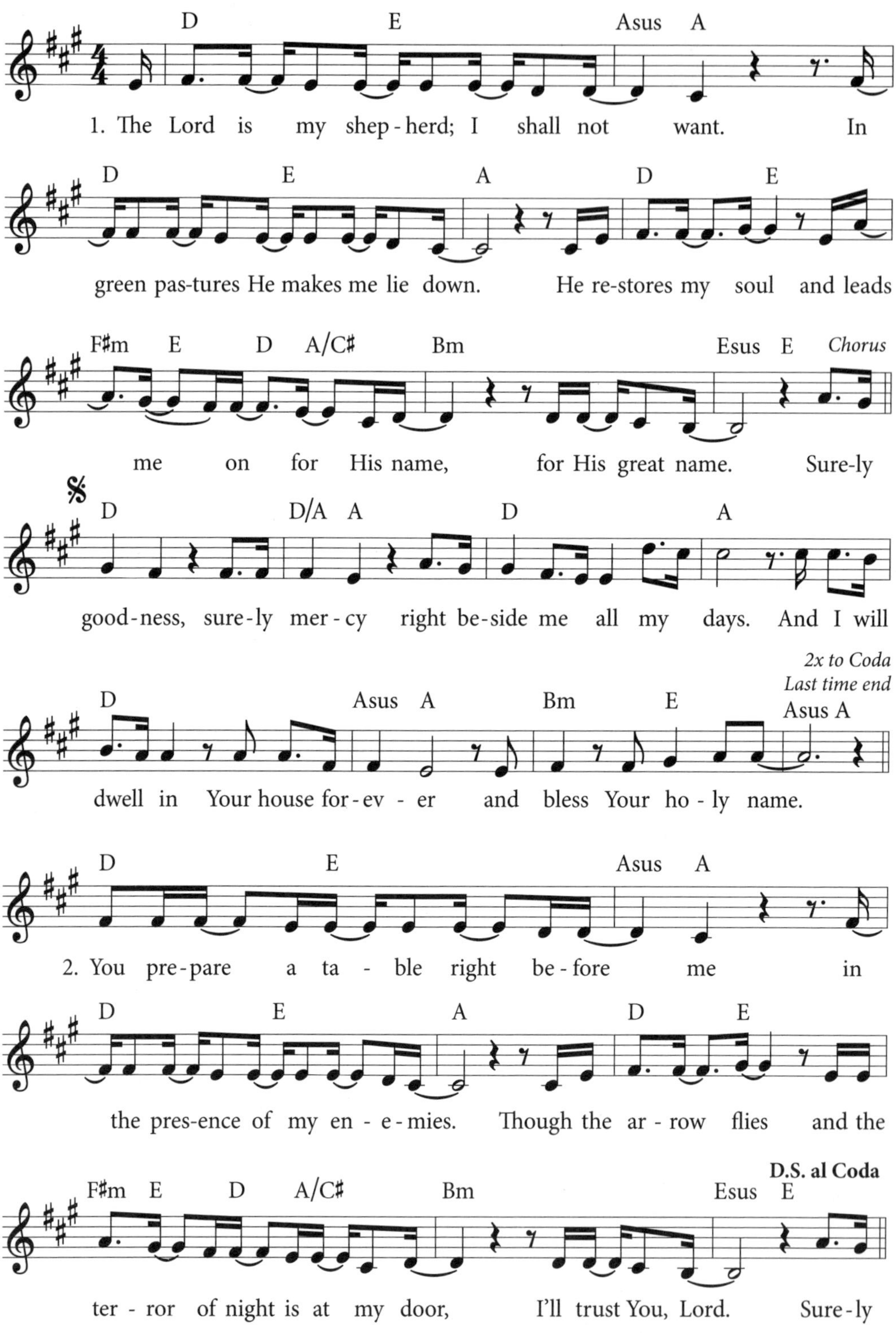

D E Asus A
1. The Lord is my shep-herd; I shall not want. In
D E A D E
green pas-tures He makes me lie down. He re-stores my soul and leads
F♯m E D A/C♯ Bm Esus E
Chorus
me on for His name, for His great name. Sure-ly
D D/A A D A
good-ness, sure-ly mer-cy right be-side me all my days. And I will
2x to Coda
Last time end
D Asus A Bm E Asus A
dwell in Your house for-ev-er and bless Your ho-ly name.
D E Asus A
2. You pre-pare a ta-ble right be-fore me in
D E A D E
the pres-ence of my en-e-mies. Though the ar-row flies and the
D.S. al Coda
F♯m E D A/C♯ Bm Esus E
ter-ror of night is at my door, I'll trust You, Lord. Sure-ly

**Coda**

And e-ven though I walk through the val-ley of the shad-ow of death, I will fear no e - vil.

And e-ven though I walk through the val-ley of the shad-ow of death, You are on my side. And e-ven though I walk through the val-ley of the shad-ow of death, I will fear no e - vil. And e-ven though I walk through the val-ley of the shad-ow of death,

*to Chorus*

You are on my side. Sure - ly

# My Soul Will Wait (Psalm 62)

1. When the en - e - my sur - rounds and my heart grows faint with-
2. You're my strong-hold and my shield, in the midst of ev - 'ry
3. This is love I can't ex - plain, this is mer - cy un - re -

in, when the dark - ness o - ver-whelms and my fears are
threat, though the wick - ed nev - er yield they will van - ish
served, through Your sac - ri - fice so great I have peace that's

press - ing in, I will trust in You, O Lord, in the
like a breath, yes, I know the out - come's sure, Sa - tan's
un - de - served, for the bat - tle has been won, and I

si - lence I will wait, I will stand up - on Your Word.
e - vil plans will fail, in Your pow - er I'm se - cure. You're my
fear no shame or loss, now the sting of death is gone.

sol-id rock and my sal-va-tion, my stead-fast hope that won't be shak-en, my

*1st time to verse 2*

soul will wait, my soul will wait for You. You're my

Words and Music: Keaton Bunting and Bob Kauflin © 2022 Sovereign Grace Praise

com-fort when I feel for-sak-en, my ref-uge and my sure foun-

*1st time to verse 3*
*2nd time to Tag*

da-tion, my soul will wait, my soul will wait for You.

Pour-ing out our hearts be - fore You, we will trust in You.

Per - fect Sav - ior, strong De - fend - er, we will trust in You.

# It Is Well with My Soul

C     F/C   G/C    C

1. When peace like a riv - er at - tend - eth my way,
2. Though Sa - tan should buf - fet, though tri - als should come,
3. My sin— oh, the bliss of this glo - ri - ous thought!
4. And Lord, haste the day when my faith shall be sight,

Am     Dsus    D   Gsus   G    C     F

when sor - rows like sea bil - lows roll, what - ev - er my lot,
let this blest as - sur - ance con - trol: that Christ has re - gard -
My sin, not in part, but the whole, is nailed to the cross,
the clouds be rolled back as a scroll; the trump shall re - sound

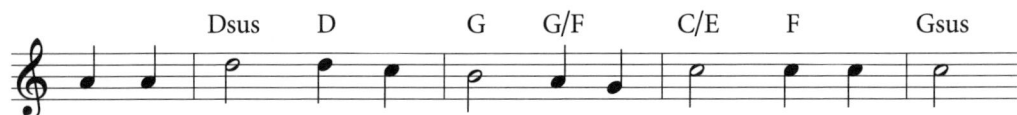

Dsus    D     G   G/F    C/E   F     Gsus

Thou hast taught me to say, "It is well, it is well
ed my help - less es - tate, and has shed His own blood
and I bear it no more; praise the Lord, praise the Lord,
and the Lord shall de - scend; ev - en so, it is well

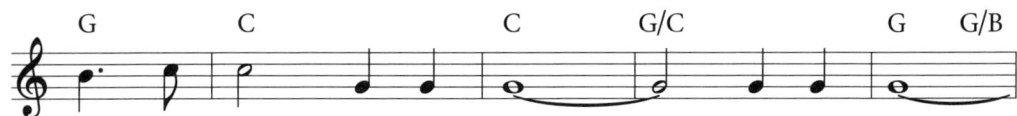

G     C       C   G/C     G   G/B

with my soul."
for my soul. It is well_____ with my soul;____
O my soul!
with my soul.

C    C/E   F      C/G   G     C

___ it is well, it is well with my soul!

Words: Horatio G. Spafford, 1876
Music: Philip P. Bliss, 1876          VILLE DU HAVRE

# Come, Thou Fount

1. Come, Thou Fount of ev - 'ry bless-ing; tune my heart to sing Thy grace;
2. Here I raise mine Eb - e - ne - zer: hith - er by Thy help I'm come,
3. Oh to grace how great a debt - or dai - ly I'm con-strained to be!
4. Oh that day when, free from sin - ning, I shall see Thy love - ly face;

streams of mer - cy, nev - er ceas-ing, call for songs of loud-est praise.
and I hope by Thy good pleas-ure safe - ly to ar - rive at home.
Let Thy good-ness like a fet - ter, bind my wan-d'ring heart to Thee.
clothed then in my blood-washed lin - en, how I'll sing Thy sov-'reign grace!

Teach me some me - lo-dious son - net, sung by flam - ing tongues a - bove;
Je - sus sought me when a stran - ger wan-d'ring from the fold of God.
Prone to wan - der, Lord, I feel it, prone to leave the God I love;
Come, my Lord, no long-er tar - ry, take my ran-somed soul a - way;

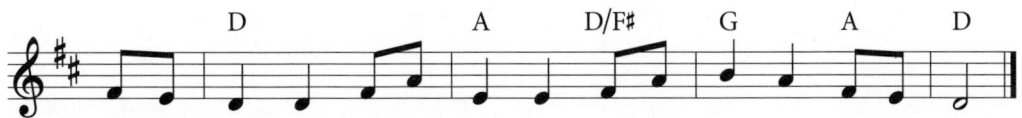

praise the mount! I'm fixed up - on it, mount of Thy re - deem-ing love.
He to res - cue me from dan - ger, in - ter - posed His pre-cious blood.
here's my heart, Lord, take and seal it, seal it for Thy courts a - bove!
send Thine an - gels now to car - ry me to realms of end-less day.

Words: Robert Robinson, 1758

Music: J. Wyeth's *Repository of Sacred Music*, Part II, 1813

NETTLETON

87 87 D

# Jesus Lives and So Shall I

1. Je - sus lives, and so shall I. Death, thy sting is gone for-
2. Je - sus lives, though once He died. In the ground He was for-
3. Je - sus lives, and reigns su - preme, and His king - dom still re-
4. Je - sus lives, I know full well. Naught from Him my heart can

ev - er! He who bowed His head to die, lives, the
sak - en. Yet, the stone was rolled a - side! How the
main - ing, I shall al - so be with Him, ev - er
sev - er, life, nor death, nor pow'rs of hell, joy, nor

bands of death to sev - er. He shall raise me from the dust;
gates of hell were shak - en! Death o - beys Him, yes, it must;
liv - ing, ev - er reign - ing. God has prom - ised. He is just;
grief, hence-forth for - ev - er. None of all His saints is lost;

Je - sus is my hope and trust. Je - sus is my hope and trust.

Words: Christian Gellert; tr. John Lang, alt.; st. 2 Erik Dewar © 2016 Glory & Gladness Music
Music: Erik Dewar © 2016 Glory & Gladness Music

# All Things

D           A

1. When my heart was cold and life - less and I wan - dered in
2. Though the en - e - my is might - y, and a thou - sand fall
3. Till the day You come in pow - er or I reach my fi -

D/F# G D/F# G    D

my blind - ness, You pur - sued me. And be - fore the world
be - side me, You de - fend me. When the wil - der - ness
- nal hour, You will keep me. You're the Au - thor of

A    D/F# G Bm

was breath - ing, You had cho - sen to re - deem me, for You loved me,
seems end - less, and I feel the weight of dark - ness, You are with me,
my sto - ry, You are faith - ful, You are for me, I will praise You,

Asus    D    A

Lord, You love me.
You are with me. I know You are work - ing, You are work - ing all things,
I will praise You.

D/F# G Bm A    D

all things for Your glo - ry and my good. Lord, You will ac - com - plish

A   D/F# G A D

ev' - ry-thing You prom - ised, all things for Your glo - ry and my good.

Words and Music: Nathan Stiff and David Zimmer © 2024 Sovereign Grace Praise

# On That Day

1. I be-lieve in Christ, ris-en from the dead. He
2. What a bless-ed hope, though now tired and worn. We

now reigns vic-to-ri-ous, His king-dom knows no end.
will spend e-ter-ni-ty a-round our Sav-ior's throne.

Through His res-ur-rec-tion, death has lost its hold.
Though we grieve our loss-es, we grieve not in vain.

I know on that fi-nal day, I'll rise as Je-sus rose.
For we know our crown of glo-ry waits be-yond the grave.

*Chorus*

On that day we will see You shin-ing bright-er than the sun. On that day we will know You as we lift our voice as one. Till that day,

Words and Music: Scott Lavender, Jonny Robinson, Rich Robinson, Nigel Hendroff, and Michael Farren

we will praise You for Your nev - er end - ing grace.

And we will keep on sing - ing on that glo-ri - ous day.

*Bridge*

Hal - le - lu - jah, what a day it will be! For at home with You, my

joy is com - plete. As I run in - to Your arms o - pen wide,

I will see my Fa-ther who is wait-ing for me.

My Fa-ther who is wait-ing for me.

# Sing

**C**

1. Did you draw a breath as the dawn a - woke, and does your
2. Has the Fa - ther's love filled your long - ing heart with grace for
3. Has the Son of God died to take a - way your sin and
4. On the fi - nal day when the Lord on high re - turns in

**G**     **C/E**     **F**

heart still beat? Is the might - y Word of the liv - ing God
ev - 'ry need? Come and lay your bur-dens at Je - sus' feet
set you free? Has the Con - quer - or tram-pled o - ver death?
maj - es - ty, we will bow in won-der be - fore the Lamb

**C/E**     **F**     **G**     **C**

up - hold - ing you? Then sing, O sing. *to v. 2*
and find new strength to sing, O sing!
Is Christ en - throned? Then sing, O sing!
and ev - er - more the saints will sing!

**F**     **Am7**     **G**     **F**  **Am7**  **G**

Morn-ing and eve - ning, ev-'ry-thing breath-ing must sing, O sing!

**F**     **Am7**     **G**     **F**  **Am7**  **G**     **C**

All of cre-a - tion rise up and praise the King of kings and sing!

Words and Music: Nathan Stiff and David Zimmer © 2024 Sovereign Grace Praise

# Almost Home

1. Don't drop a sin-gle an-chor, we're al-most home; through ev-'ry toil and dan-ger, we're al-most home. How man-y pil-grim saints have be-fore us gone? No stop-ping now— we're al-most home. *to v. 2*

2. The prom-ised land is call-ing, we're al-most home; and not a tear shall fall then, we're al-most home. Make read-y now your souls, for that king-dom come. No turn-ing back— we're al-most home.

3. This jour-ney ours to-geth-er, we're al-most home; un-to that great for-ev-er, we're al-most home. What song a-new we'll sing 'round that hap-py throne. Come, faint of heart, we're al-most home.

4. This life is just a va-por, we're al-most home; that sun is set-ting yon-der, we're al-most home. Take cour-age for this dark-ness shall break to dawn; oh lift your eyes, we're al-most home.

Al-most home, we're al-most home. So, press on t'ward that bless-ed shore, oh praise the Lord! We're al-most home.

Words and Music: Matt Boswell, Matt Papa, and Lauren Papa © 2021 Getty Music Hymns and Songs

# Amazing Grace

| | | | | | | | | |
|---|---|---|---|---|---|---|---|---|
| 1. A | - maz | - ing | grace! | how | sweet | the | sound | that |
| 2. 'Twas | grace | that | taught | my | heart | to | fear, | and |
| 3. Through | man | - y | dan - | gers, | toils, | and | snares, | I |
| 4. The | Lord | has | prom - | ised | good | to | me, | His |
| 5. The | earth | shall | soon | dis - | solve | like | snow; | the |
| 6. When | we've | been | there | ten | thou - | sand | years, | bright |

| | | | | | | | | |
|---|---|---|---|---|---|---|---|---|
| saved | a | wretch | like | me! | I | once | was | lost, but |
| grace | my | fears | re - | lieved; | how | pre - | cious | did that |
| have | al - | read - | y | come; | 'tis | grace | has | brought me |
| word | my | hope | se - | cures; | He | will | my | Shield and |
| sun | for - | bear | to | shine; | but | God, | who | called me |
| shin - | ing | as | the | sun, | we've | no | less | days to |

| | | | | | | | |
|---|---|---|---|---|---|---|---|
| now | am | found, | was | blind, | but | now | I | see. |
| grace | ap - | pear | the | hour | I | first | be - | lieved! |
| safe | thus | far, | and | grace | will | lead | me | home. |
| Por - | tion | be | as | long | as | life | en - | dures. |
| here | be - | low, | will | be | for - | ev - | er | mine. |
| sing | God's | praise | than | when | we'd | first | be - | gun. |

Words: st. 1–5 John Newton, 1779; st. 6 anonymous
Music: *Columbian Harmony*, 1829

NEW BRITAIN
CM